Kita's KITCHEN

STRESS-FREE RECIPES FOR MEMORABLE MEALS

MARKITA ADAIR-CRUDUP

Kita's KITCHEN
STRESS-FREE RECIPES FOR MEMORABLE MEALS

Copyright © 2023 by Kita's Kitchen
Printed in USA

All rights reserved. No part of this publication may be reproduced, distributed, or transmitted in any form or by any means, including photocopying, recording, or other electronic or mechanical methods, without the prior written permission of the publisher, except in the case of brief quotations embodied in critical reviews and certain other noncommercial uses permitted by copyright law.

This cookbook is a work of original authorship and is protected by the copyright laws of the United States and other countries. The author and publisher have made every effort to ensure the accuracy of the information herein. However, the information contained in this cookbook is sold without warranty, either express or implied, including, but not limited to, the implied warranties of merchantability and fitness for a particular purpose.

The recipes and information in this cookbook are intended for personal use and enjoyment. The author and publisher are not responsible for any adverse effects or consequences resulting from the use of the recipes or information contained in this book. It is the responsibility of the reader to ensure that they are following all safety guidelines, including those related to food allergies and dietary restrictions.

Library of Congress Control Number: 2023920151
ISBN: 979-8-9891085-1-0 (Hardback)

Cover design - Premier Branding & Marketing Solutions
Editing, Interior layout and design - Purposely Booked Publishing
Photography - Picture Play Media & Premier Branding & Marketing Solutions

For information about permission to reproduce selections from this cookbook, please contact: Chefkita@fromkitaskitchen.com.

Visit our website at kitaskitchen.com.

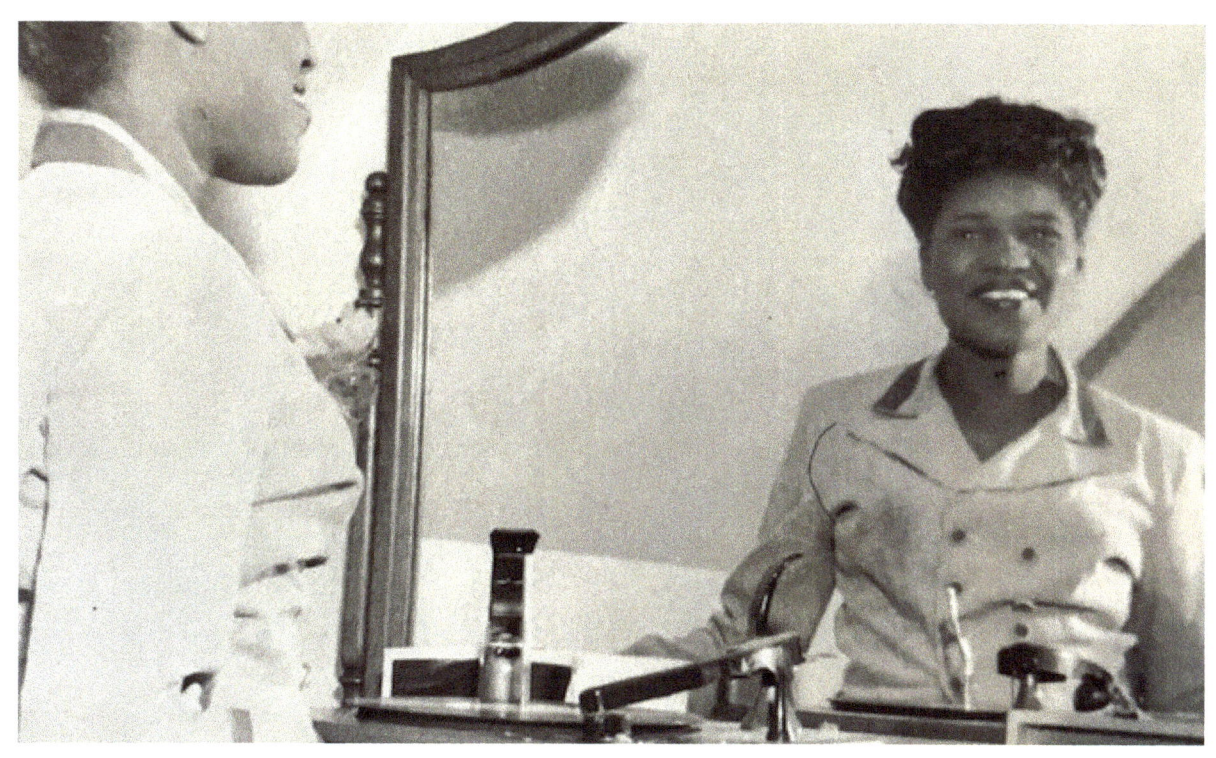

The memories of you are treasures I hold dear. From your wet kisses to your distinctive laugh, your presence is missed greatly. This book is dedicated to you grandma.

Foreword

Every once in a while in an educator's career; definitely not often enough, a teacher stumbles across a student that makes them say, "THIS is why I became a teacher!" It may not be obvious right away; it rarely is, but at some point, THAT STUDENT gets you excited to stay up late grading assignments, and they challenge you to make sure that you have the answers to ALL of the questions You know they're going to ask. Markita Adair was THAT STUDENT!

Vertically challenged, bespectacled, African American, and female, Ms. Adair came to me at Vance Granville Community College determined to become a chef! I'm pretty sure my first impressions weren't terribly enthusiastic. First impressions are notoriously flawed, and mine were no exception!

Kita (she'll ALWAYS be Markita to me) wasn't my best student, but she certainly wasn't my worst. She was hardworking, energetic, and opinionated (aka, stubborn), with a constant smile and affable personality that made you want to see her succeed!!!

Fast-forward a decade plus, through time, distance and the magic of social media, my former student has become my friend. I've watched her personal life and career blossom from a distance. She's grown older and wiser, gone from Ms. to Mrs., and preceded the title of Chef with Mom. Kita has done all of this in a way that makes me proud to think I might have had a little influence on her success!

Fast forward to today, and I have been graced with the honor of being asked to author the foreword to this work. When a country girl from Henderson, North Carolina, sets out to write a book about cooking, expectations often fall on the obvious: southern cooking. That's right, another tome extolling the virtues of grits, fried chicken, and biscuits. Remember what I said earlier about flawed first impressions? Don't get ahead of yourself! I'll bet you even money that Kita's about to surprise me yet again!

I, for one, am thoroughly anxious to turn the pages of Kita's new book. As my student, she often found ways to turn tradition on its head; bringing unique, often startling interpretations to recipes, which, over the years, have come to be labeled traditional, at best, and at worst, boring. I know, for a fact, that Kita will bring a classical culinary education to the pages of this work because I had the good fortune to have assisted in laying the foundation for that education.

With that said, allow me to remind you that Markita has always been full of surprises and I spent much of my time as her teacher watching her exceed my expectations. I expect nothing less than that here. I fully anticipate casual readers, enthusiastic amateur chefs, and perhaps even an old culinary arts instructor or two, to be thoroughly surprised and entertained. More importantly, I expect to learn something new and exciting! Reader, waste no more time with this foreword! Read on and enjoy what I am sure will be a book that will have us all running into the kitchen to enjoy the unique flavors of one of my favorite students!

Chef Joseph Brown

Basic Muffin 4

Quiche Lorraine 6

Sweet Potato Biscuits 8
with Maple Bourbon Butter

Buttermilk Biscuits 9

Andouille Sausage Gravy 9

Caramel Skillet Apples 11

Fruit Salad 12
with Basil-Lime Syrup

Breakfast Burritos 13

Sweet Potato Waffles 15
with Candied Pecans

Strawberry Cheesecake French Toast 16

Best Breakfast Potatoes 17

Cheesy Breakfast Souffle 17

Sweet Potato & Pepper Hash 18

Let's Do BRUNCH

Pop's Pork & Poultry Rub 25

My Husband's Rib(s) 25

Roasted Chicken & Vegetables 27

Bacon & Cider Brussels Sprouts 27

Smoked Gouda Mac & Cheese 28

Chicken Enchilada Soup 29

Corn, Bacon & Tater Chowder 30

Summer Squash Casserole 31

Easy Like Sunday Roast 31

Homemade Marinara 32

Roasted Vegetable Lasagna 34

Shrimp & Asparagus Risotto 35

Greek Chicken 36

Turmeric Rice 36

Shrimp Scampi & Linguine 37

Garlic & Cheddar Drop Biscuits 39

Lulu's Sweet Potatoes 41

Hot Honey Pork Chops 42

Panko Parmesan Crusted Chicken 43

Spicy Southern Collards 45

Roasted Broccolini 45
with Lemon & Parm

Grilled Snapper with Cilantro Sauce 46

Corn Relish 46

Smokey Queso Dip 47

Corn & Tomato Salad 49
with Prosecco Vinaigrette

Sriracha Aioli 54

Napa Slaw 54

Asian Pickled Veggies 55

Korean Short Ribs 58

Sweet Chili Sauce 60

Pork Egg Rolls 60

Hoisin Pork Meatballs 61

Roasted Green Beans 62
with Ponzu

Scallion Rice 62

Sweet & Spicy Sesame Glaze 63

Thai Steak Lettuce Wraps 64

Pineapple Fried Rice 65

Kita's KFC (Korean Fried Chicken) 67

Korean Braised Potatoes 68

Gochugang Chicken & Vegetables 69

Soy-Honey Glazed Salmon 73

Asian Influences

Can I Make You a Drink?

Summer Spritz 76

Pineapple Tickle 76

Bourbon & Blackberry Lemonade 79

Peach Margarita 80

Mimosa, Anyone? 81

Sweet Endings

Coconut Vanilla Bread Pudding 90

Anglaise 91

Ginger Peach Cobbler 95
with Ginger Cream

Chocolate Chess Pie 96

Vanilla Pound Cake 97
with Blueberry-Thyme Glaze

Lavender-Lemon Cookies 99

PB, Bacon & Chocolate Chip Cookies 100

Orange Rice Pudding 101

Everyone who loves to be in the kitchen has their "go-to" brands for just about everything. The same goes for me. These are a few of the products that I use in my own kitchen.

Salt: Morton's Coarse Kosher salt is the only salt I use. Throughout most of this book, the amount of salt used is determined by your personal preferences with the exception of the measurements called for in the baking recipes. *Please note that using a different brand or type of salt may yield varying results.* Morton's is a coarse blend that has larger crystals.
Substituting iodized salt, for example, may create salty desserts.

Mayonnaise: There's no question about it…Duke's Mayo is the way to go, and it's the only mayo allowed in my kitchen. I would not suggest substituting Miracle Whip for any of these recipes. It's sweeter and has other added ingredients.

Bourbon: My bourbon of choice for cooking and baking is Jim Beam. No need to waste a lot of money on a more expensive bourbon.

Tequila: I absolutely love the Blue Nectar brand, but it's not readily available. If you can find it, great! But if not, other great options are Lunazul and Casamigos.

Flour: I love the King Arthur flour brand, but during the pandemic, I had to learn to use what was available. Martha White is a less expensive option.

Spices: I absolutely love Badia brand spices. They are of great quality without the expensive price tag. They can be found in specialty markets or most grocery stores' international section. I also use the McCormick brand as they have a wider range of spices.

I use the Mizkan brand for most of my Asian ingredients, like rice vinegar, ponzu, and mirin.

Soy Sauce: Kikkoman

Product Recommendations

In the kitchen, chefs use abbreviations when writing out recipes. To some who are not in the kitchen often, they may be a little confusing. Here's a cheat sheet to help beginners, check it out below.

Tablespoon = Tbsp
Teaspoon = tsp
Pound(s) = Lb or Lbs or #
To Taste = TT
All-Purpose Flour = APF or AP flour
Self Rising Flour = SR flour
Baking Powder = B.P.
Baking Soda = B.S.
Powdered Sugar = Confectioners Sugar = 10x

Culinary Abbreviations Guide

Introduction

Cooking is an expression of affection that requires no words. Just a little bit of soul and a whole lot of love. I grew up watching my grandmother Lula (affectionately called LuLu) and my mom in the kitchen. There were no recipe cards or cookbooks. At my grandmother's home, I watched how she carefully managed the temperature of her log burning stove to simmer stews or braise meats. My mom would prepare meals almost daily. Dinner would be done promptly at 5:30 pm, Sunday through Thursday. The only exception to this was Wednesdays because that was church night, so we ate a little earlier. Cooking for their families brought them joy, and watching them as a little girl sparked my love for being in the kitchen. I love expressing myself through food and I love sharing that with others. Anyone who has ever been to my home has been fed, whether it was a full meal or a slice of cake. Feeding others allows me to show the people in my life that they are loved and cared for. This is one of the things that gives me joy. I hope that as you go through this cookbook, you can sense that.

Here's to food, family, friends and love!

Chef Kita

Writing a cookbook has been just a dream for a very long time. At the end of 2022, I knew I finally wanted that dream to become a reality. When I first started the process, I knew two things might be difficult for me. The first was figuring out the recipes that I wanted to include. The next was breaking down those recipes into actual measurements. Measuring is not something that I regularly practice unless I'm baking. And even then, I sometimes throw that rule out of the window. When it came to choosing the recipes, I knew that I wanted them to reflect who I am. A woman born and raised in the south who is proud of her roots and who also loves Asian flavors. As a busy wife, mom, and entrepreneur, spending a ton of time in the kitchen during the week is just not possible. So with keeping that in mind, I wrote down the meals that do not require a ton of time or prep. With a few exceptions, most of these recipes can be done in 30 minutes or less. I narrowed the list down with the help of my family and framily (friends who become family). Even after the list was done and recipe testing started, the list changed several times. I believe the ones that made the cut are the perfect introduction to who I am in the kitchen.

These recipes include my husband's kind of famous pork ribs, my grandma's pineapple sweet potatoes, and some that came from other inspirations. And now, trial run after trial run, I finally have a collection of recipes my family and friends love in print. These recipes are special to me because they remind me of all the times, I've gathered with my loved ones, laughing together and making new memories. I hope you enjoy them as much as we do.

Everyone knows that I love to eat. It's a love language! My favorite meal of the day is dinner (or supper, depending on what part of the country you live in). You'll see that it's obvious given the recipes that are featured in this book. Breakfast lovers don't fret! I have a few things for you, too.

"You don't have to cook fancy or complicated masterpieces — just good food from fresh ingredients."

Julia Child

Brunch - the meal that happens somewhere between breakfast and lunch. I've entitled this section *"Let's Do Brunch"* because I prefer leisurely late-morning feasting and mimosas, but you can enjoy these recipes as early as you'd like. Whether you're gathering with friends and family on a lazy weekend morning or simply treating yourself to a mid-morning escape, brunch is the perfect occasion to indulge in a delightful fusion of breakfast and lunch flavors.

Brunch is not just about the food; it's also about creating a relaxed and inviting atmosphere. Some of my favorite tips for creating the perfect brunch setting are:

1. **Choose a Theme or Color Scheme:** Start by selecting a theme or color scheme that sets the mood. Whether it's a rustic farmhouse brunch, a chic urban gathering, or a colorful springtime theme, having a cohesive theme or color palette will help you tie everything together.
2. **Add Centerpiece Flair: A beautiful centerpiece can be the focal point of your table.** It could be a vase of fresh flowers, a collection of candles, a fruit bowl, or even a decorative tray with seasonal items. Make sure it doesn't obstruct guests' view or conversation.
3. **Consider Dietary Needs:** Even if you don't know all your guests' dietary preferences or restrictions, try to accommodate them by offering a variety of brunch dishes, including vegetarian, vegan, and gluten-free options.
4. **Keep It Neat:** I hate clutter! As the meal progresses, make sure to clear empty plates and used utensils to keep the table looking inviting.
Relax and have fun!

"Food is symbolic of love when words are inadequate."
—Alan D. Wolfelt

Basic Muffin Recipe

½ cup Melted Unsalted Butter
1 cup of White Sugar
2 Large Eggs
1 ½ tsp of Vanilla
¼ cup Sour Cream
⅓ cup of Whole Milk
2 ½ cups All-Purpose Flour
2 tsp Baking Powder
1 tsp Salt

Preheat the oven to 375 degrees. Measure ingredients and add the first six ingredients into a mixing bowl. Whisk together to blend thoroughly. Measure dry ingredients into a separate bowl. Fold dry ingredients into wet and stir in any dry mix-ins you would like. Scoop into baking cups using a 2 oz ice cream scoop. Bake for 18-20 minutes.

Variations:

Banana Nut: Omit the sour cream. Add in 1 mashed banana, 1 tsp of cinnamon and ½ c chopped walnuts or pecans.

Blueberry: Add in 1 cup frozen blueberries tossed in 2 TBSP of flour and 1 teaspoon of lemon zest.

Chocolate Chip: Stir in one cup of chocolate chips.

Cinnamon: Mix 2 tsp of cinnamon into batter and top with pearl sugar, also known as coarse sugar.

Quiche Lorraine

4 oz Cream Cheese, softened
6 large Eggs
1 small Shallot, diced
4 ounces Gruyere Cheese, grated
¾ cup Light Cream or Half & Half
8 Strips of Cooked and Chopped Bacon
Dash of Nutmeg
Salt
¼ tsp White Pepper
1 9" Pie Crust
Parchment paper
1 cup Dry Beans or Rice

Preheat the oven to 350 degrees. Place a square of parchment paper over the pie crust and pour the beans or rice into the parchment paper. Bake the crust for 15 minutes and remove from the oven. Lightly sauté the shallot with a bit of olive oil in a pan for 1-2 minutes. Blend cream cheese, eggs, and cream until smooth. In a bowl, combine egg mixture, shallots, cheese and bacon. Add salt, pepper, and a dash of nutmeg. Set pie crust on a sheet pan and pour mixture into the crust. Bake for 45-50 minutes. Remove from the oven and allow the quiche to cool for 15 minutes. It will continue to set as it cools. Serve slightly warm.

The Story

I remember the first time I tried to make biscuits from scratch. My grandma and mom made it look so easy! I gathered my flour, shortening, buttermilk, and salt. I preheated the oven and started to work my dough. I punched my biscuits out and put them in the oven feeling proud of myself. When the timer went off, I pulled my biscuits out of the oven, but I immediately knew something was wrong. The only thing that looked right was that they were round. My biscuits looked like pale, flat hockey pucks. And they felt like them, too! My mom and I laughed at those disastrous little bricks, and it was a while before I tried again. My biscuit making skills have tremendously improved, and I could turn out a soft, fluffy biscuit in my sleep. I think my ancestors would be proud.

Sweet Potato Biscuits
with Bourbon Maple Butter

I contemplated whether I would add a biscuit recipe. Every southern cookbook has one. After all, what is more southern than a perfectly baked, fluffy biscuit? After much thought, I figured I would offer both a traditional recipe and give you all a little something different. Whip the Bourbon Butter together while you wait for the biscuits to bake. These biscuits are sure to add something special to brunch or dinner!

3 cups Self-Rising Flour, plus more as needed
½ cup cold Vegetable Shortening
1 large Sweet Potato, Roasted, Mashed, and Cooled completely (about 1 ½ cups)
1 Tbsp Sugar
¼ tsp salt
¾ cup cold Buttermilk

Bourbon Maple Butter

1 stick Softened, Salted Butter
¾ cup Bourbon
2 Tbsp Maple Syrup
¼ tsp Salt

Preheat the oven to 425 degrees. Mix dry ingredients into a bowl. Add the cold vegetable shortening to the dry ingredients. Using your hands, work the shortening into the flour mixture using a massage-like motion. Continue to do this until the mixture has a sandy consistency. Add in buttermilk and sweet potato and gently work into flour to form a dough. Sprinkle a clean surface with flour and turn the biscuit dough onto the flour. Pat or roll out the dough into a circle that's about ½ inch thick and then fold in half. Repeat this step once more. Roll or pat out the dough until it's once again about ½ inch thick and punch out circles using a biscuit cutter 3" in diameter. Place biscuits side by side on a baking sheet lined with a piece of parchment paper. Chill biscuits in the fridge for at least 15 minutes. While you are chilling the biscuits, you can begin reducing the bourbon. Place bourbon in a small saucepan and bring to a boil. When the bourbon has reduced by half of the original amount, remove from heat, and allow to cool in the refrigerator. Bake the biscuits for 15-18 minutes. While the biscuits are baking, whip the butter, bourbon reduction, and syrup for 5 minutes to combine well. When biscuits are out, brush them with the bourbon butter and enjoy!

Buttermilk Biscuits
with Andouille Gravy

My family could eat these any time of the year, but my favorite time to make them is when the weather turns cool. There is something wonderful and cozy about a fresh from the oven biscuit during the colder months. I love them with a nice spread of blackberry jam or covered in sausage gravy.

2 ¾ cups Self-Rising Flour, plus more for dusting
½ cup cold Vegetable Shortening
2 tsp Sugar
¼ tsp salt
1 cup cold Buttermilk
4 Tbsp melted butter

Preheat the oven to 425 degrees. Mix dry ingredients into a bowl. Add the cold vegetable shortening to the dry ingredients. Using your hands, work the shortening into the flour mixture using a massage-like motion. Continue to do this until the mixture has a sandy consistency. Pour in buttermilk and gently work into flour to form a dough. Sprinkle a clean surface with flour and turn biscuit dough onto the flour. Pat out dough into a circle that's about ½ inch thick and then fold in half and then fold once more. Pat this out until the dough is again about ½ inch thick and punch out circles using a biscuit cutter 3" in diameter. Line biscuits on a baking sheet lined with a piece of parchment paper. Chill biscuits in the fridge for at least 15 minutes. Put the biscuits into the oven and bake for 14-15 minutes. When biscuits are out, brush them with the melted butter and enjoy.

Andouille Sausage Gravy

4 ounces Andouille Sausage
¼ cup Yellow Onion, small dice
1 tsp minced garlic
2 ½ Tbsp AP Flour
1 ¼ cups Milk
1 tsp Paprika
½ tsp dried Thyme
Salt & Pepper

Chop and brown sausage in a large skillet over medium-high heat for 3-4 minutes. Add in diced onion and garlic and continue to cook for 1 minute. Sprinkle flour over sausage and onions. Cook mixture for 2-3 minutes, stirring frequently to keep flour from sticking to the bottom of the pan. Pour in milk while stirring. Turn the heat down to medium-low and stir in paprika and thyme. Let simmer for 5 minutes and season to taste with salt & black pepper.

Skillet Caramel Apples

This dish was inspired by a similar dish I once had at a restaurant in Durham, N.C. I came up with my own version of it after I developed an allergy to fresh apples, and the only way, I can eat them is if the apples are cooked. This satisfies my sweet tooth and allows me to enjoy the fruit I love so much. You can use any firm apple you'd like for this recipe, but I like using honey crisp or opal varieties.

1-pound Apples, cored & cut into slices about ¾ inch thick
1 ½ Tbsp Unsalted Butter
1/3 cup Brown Sugar
1 tsp Vanilla Extract
1 tsp Saigon Cinnamon

In a cast iron or other skillet, melt butter and add apples & brown sugar. Stir to combine. When the mixture begins to bubble, add vanilla and cinnamon. Stir and cook for **6-8** minutes until mixture is bubbly. Apples will still have a slight bite. If you want softer apples, cook for **2-3** minutes more.

Fruit Salad
with Basil-Lime Syrup

2 cups seedless Watermelon, diced
1 large Mango, removed from flesh and diced
2 Dragon Fruit, peeled and diced
½ of a Pineapple, diced
3 Kiwi's, peeled and diced

For the syrup:
¾ cup Honey
¼ Water
1 Tbsp chopped Basil
Zest of 1 small Lime

Place honey and water for the syrup in a small saucepan and bring to a light boil. Whisk to combine and remove the pan from the heat. Allow to cool before adding in basil and lime zest. Pour the syrup over the fruit and mix gently to coat.

Garnish with more basil if desired, and serve.

This fresh fruit salad is perfect for a spring or summer brunch. You can swap out fruits to make it your own!

Breakfast Burritos

The great thing about these burritos is that they are so easy to do, and you can freeze them ahead of time to prepare for a busy week. Simply reheat in the microwave or oven for a quick breakfast.

First step is to choose your meat if using:

8 Bacon Strips, cooked and chopped
8 oz Sausage, cooked and crumbled
1 cup Ham, chopped

For the filling:

1 Jalapeno, diced
½ cup diced Bell Pepper (use any bell pepper that you prefer)
¼ cup Yellow Onion, diced
6 large Eggs
¼ cup Half & Half
Salt & Pepper
1 cup Colby Jack cheese
4 Flour Tortillas, Burrito
Oil

Preheat oven to 350 degrees.

Blend eggs and Half & Half, set aside. In a pan, add a drizzle of oil, and diced peppers and onions. Sprinkle it with a bit of salt & pepper and sauté for 4-5 minutes on medium heat. Add egg mixture and season with salt. Move eggs around with a rubber spatula, being sure to scrape bottom to keep eggs from sticking to the pan. When your eggs are cooked to your liking, remove the pan from heat.

Place tortillas on a baking sheet or large cutting board. Add your protein choice across the center of each tortilla. Follow this with the cheese divided evenly amongst the tortillas. Next, add your egg mixture dividing them between the tortillas. Finally, it's time to wrap your breakfast burritos. Fold in the sides and then wrap from the bottom and away from you. With seam side down brush the tops of the burritos with a little olive oil and bake for 8-9 minutes. If you are freezing, let the burritos cool completely before placing them in a freezer bag.

Sweet Potato Waffles
with Candied Pecans

2 cups Self-Rising Flour
1 tsp Baking Soda
½ tsp Salt
1 tsp Cinnamon
½ tsp Nutmeg
3 Tbsp Brown Sugar
2 large Eggs
1 cup mashed Sweet Potato
1 cup Whole Milk
1 tsp Vanilla Extract
¼ cup Melted Butter

Preheat a waffle iron. Place the first six ingredients in a bowl and stir to combine. Next, place the eggs, milk, vanilla, and sweet potato into a bowl and whisk well. Stir the wet ingredients into the dry and then add butter. Let the mixture sit for 10 minutes before using.

Depending on the size of your waffle iron, pour 1/3 to 1/2 a cup of the waffle mix into the cavity and cook per the directions of your iron. Sprinkle with candied pecans and serve with maple syrup.

Candied Pecans

This is a versatile treat that can be used to top sundaes and oatmeal, sprinkled into granola, and more! I use these candied nuts as a crunchy, sweet topping for my sweet potato waffles.

1 pound Pecan Halves
1/3 cup + 1 Tbsp White Sugar
1 tsp Cinnamon
½ tsp Nutmeg
1/8 tsp Cayenne Pepper
2 tsp Water
1 tsp Vanilla
1 Egg White

Preheat the oven to 250 degrees. Place all ingredients in a bowl and mix well, making sure that the pecans are thoroughly coated. Place the coated nuts on a baking sheet and bake for 30 minutes. Stir the nuts and continue to bake for another 30 minutes. Remove from the oven and let cool.

Strawberry Cheesecake French Toast

This delicious treat is one of my favorites to eat and serve! It requires a little more preparation than most of my breakfast items, but it is so worth the extra time. You don't want to use fresh bread for this recipe because it won't yield the desired results. No one wants to eat soggy French toast. It's okay to let your bread dry out a bit by laying the slices on a baking sheet and covering them with a paper towel or a clean kitchen towel.

For the toast:
8 slices of Brioche, about 1" thick
¾ cup Cream
5 large Eggs
¼ tsp Nutmeg
1 tsp Vanilla
1 Tbsp Sugar
Pinch of Salt
1/3 Unsalted Butter, melted

For the Berries:
1 ½ cups of Strawberries, cleaned and sliced
1 tsp Lemon Juice
1/3 cup Sugar

For the Cream Cheese:
8 oz Cream Cheese
1 tsp Vanilla Extract
¼ cup Powdered Sugar
1 Tbsp Cream

Blend ingredients for cream cheese and set aside. In a small saucepan, combine the ingredients for the strawberry sauce, stirring to combine. Bring to a boil and then turn down to a simmer. Let the sauce simmer for 15-20 minutes, stirring occasionally. The sauce will continue to thicken as it cools.

Now for the toast! Blend heavy cream, eggs, nutmeg, vanilla, sugar, and salt in a shallow baking dish. Preheat the griddle if you have one, to 350 degrees. If using a skillet, heat over medium high heat. Dip bread into egg mixture, coating both sides allowing the bread to soak up some of the custard. Brush griddle or pan with melted butter and fry slices until crusty and golden, and then flip to cook the other side. To serve, place 1-2 slices on a plate and top with a dollop of cream cheese and a big spoon of strawberry sauce.

Best Breakfast Potatoes

1 LB Yukon Gold Potatoes, diced into ½" cubes
1 small Red Bell Pepper, diced
½ Onion, large dice
1 tsp Smoked Paprika
¼ tsp Thyme
1 Tbsp Canola Oil
Salt & Pepper
Parsley, chopped for garnish, optional

To begin, you will want to parboil potatoes to soften them up a bit. Wash and dice potatoes. Bring to a boil in a pot of water and cook for 8-10 minutes. Drain well.

Preheat a large skillet on medium heat with a Tbsp of canola oil. I prefer to use a cast iron skillet, but you can use whatever you have. Once your pan is ready add onions, peppers, and potatoes. Add paprika, thyme, salt, and pepper. Sauté until potatoes are golden brown and vegetables have softened slightly for about 5-6 minutes. Serve directly from the skillet or place into a serving bowl and garnish with parsley.

Cheesy Breakfast Souffle

There's a restaurant that I'm sure some of you may know about that sells breakfast souffle. They're delicious but they always sell out so quickly! I knew I had to recreate these at home. I like to have mine with a side of fresh fruit and a homemade latte. I hope that you enjoy these as much as I do.

4 large Eggs
1/3 cup Cream
1/2 cup shredded Gruyere Cheese
½ cup Parmesan Cheese
1 package Puff Pastry sheet, thawed
Dash of Nutmeg
½ tsp Salt
¼ tsp White Pepper
Chives, minced (optional)
4 Ramekins- 5"

Preheat the oven to 400 degrees. Spray tart pans with nonstick spray. Roll out puff pastry and cut into 4 equal size squares. Place the squares into ramekins and press in lightly. Poke holes into the bottom using a fork. Mix eggs, cream, nutmeg, salt and pepper until well blended. Add in the cheeses. Divide egg mixture evenly among the tart pans. Fold in corners of pastry. Place all of the ramekins on a baking sheet. Bake for 30-35 minutes. Garnish with minced chives if using.

Sweet Potato and Pepper Hash

3 large Sweet Potatoes, peeled and large dice (about 1 inch cubes)
2 Red Bell peppers, diced
2 Jalapenos, diced
1 Tbsp minced Garlic
2 tsp Paprika
Olive Oil
Salt & Pepper
1-2 Tbsp chopped Parsley

Place a sheet pan in your oven and preheat the oven to 425 degrees. Drizzle cubed sweet potatoes with 3-4 tablespoons of olive oil, paprika, salt, and pepper and toss to coat well. Dump sweet potatoes into a hot pan and arrange in a single layer. Roast for 15 minutes then stir. Repeat this step 2 more times in 15-minute increments. This helps the potatoes cook and develop a crust without burning. After stirring for the final time, add diced peppers and minced garlic. Stir to incorporate. Your potatoes should be done or almost done at this point. If they need a few more minutes, continue to roast for another 10 minutes. In a large bowl mix the potatoes with pepper mixture. Transfer back to the skillet or serving bowl and sprinkle with parsley to garnish and serve.

"Good food is very often, even most often, simple food."

Anthony Bourdain

Time for a Dinner Party!!

One of my absolute favorite things to do is host friends for dinner. I get excited about menu planning and the theme. When hosting in your home there are a few things that you should think about to make a memorable evening. First? Music. Music sets the tone for the evening; it should be heard but not so loud that it takes away from the conversation. Been a while since you've had a moment to catch up? Play some smooth jazz. Couples' night in? May I suggest acoustic R&B tunes. The soundtrack is just as important as the meal. Second, your menu should reflect the theme for the evening. If you're hosting a game night, something fun like a taco bar would be a hit. Finally, you must have beverages. Whether you are serving cocktails or mocktails, wine or lemonade, make it fancy. Choose decorative glasses, pitchers and/or garnishes. Thoughtfully chosen details can make the evening special. Pull out that special platter or the decorative plates you never use, light some candles, and turn on some music. Create a night that your guests will remember for years to come.

Dinner Bell

My husband's ribs are requested at nearly every function that we host. They are full of flavor and so delicious! I decided to have a little fun with word play when naming this recipe. I'm sure you have heard the story of how Eve was formed from one of Adam's ribs. She was bone of his bone and flesh of his flesh. I like to think that God made me especially for my husband and vice versa. I am my husband's rib.

My Husband's Rib(s)

My Husband's Rib(s)

2-3 LB Slab of Spareribs
2 Tbsp Spicy Brown Mustard (we tested with Gulden's)
Ced's pork & poultry rub
Aluminum Foil
½ stick Unsalted Butter

A variety of cooking methods can be used for ribs. My husband's preferred method is to smoke them low and slow. You can also use a grill or just pop them in the oven. In this book I chose to use the oven method for its ease. To achieve a smokey flavor in the oven you can add a bit of liquid smoke directly to the ribs.

Ced's Pork & Poultry Rub

The blend my husband uses whenever he smokes or grills chicken and pork. It's the perfect balance of sweet, smokey and spicy!

⅓ cup Brown Sugar
1 Tbsp Salt
1 tsp Garlic Powder
2 tsp Chili Powder
1 tsp Onion Powder
1 tsp Pepper
1 tsp Cayenne Pepper
1 Tbsp Smoked Paprika

Combine all of the pices and mix well.

My Husband's Rib(s)

2-3 LB Slab of Spareribs
2 Tbsp Spicy Brown Mustard (we tested with Gulden's)
Ced's pork & poultry rub
Aluminum Foil
½ stick Unsalted Butter

A variety of cooking methods can be used for ribs. My husband's preferred method is to smoke them low and slow. You can also use a grill or just pop them in the oven. In this book I chose to use the oven method for its ease. To achieve a smokey flavor in the oven you can add a bit of liquid smoke directly to the ribs.

Ced's Pork & Poultry Rub

The blend my husband uses whenever he smokes or grills chicken and pork. It's the perfect balance of sweet, smokey and spicy!

⅓ cup Brown Sugar
1 Tbsp Salt
1 tsp Garlic Powder
2 tsp Chili Powder
1 tsp Onion Powder
1 tsp Pepper
1 tsp Cayenne Pepper
1 Tbsp Smoked Paprika

Combine all of the pices and mix well.

Roasted Chicken & Vegetables

2 LBs Bone-In Chicken (Larger pieces like breast, thighs and legs work well for this recipe)
3 medium sized Yukon Gold Potatoes, diced into large cubes
1 large Sweet Potato, peeled and diced into large cubes
1 large Red Onion, cut into 4 wedges
3 Carrots, peeled and cut into 1 ½ inch pieces
2 Tbsp Minced Garlic
1 Tbsp Smoked Paprika
1 tsp Dry Thyme
2 Tbsp Fresh Parsley, chopped plus more for garnish
4 Tbsp Mayonnaise
2 Tbsp Salt
2 tsp Pepper

Preheat the oven to 375 degrees. Add the vegetables to a large bowl along with the garlic, 1 teaspoon of paprika, ½ teaspoon of thyme, 1 tablespoon of parsley, 1 tablespoon of mayo, salt, and pepper. Mix well and place in a large baking dish.

For the chicken, mix the remaining ingredients along with salt and pepper. Massage into chicken being sure to work under skin as well. Arrange chicken on top of the vegetables. Roast for an hour. Check the tempaterature of the chicken at the 45 minute mark to test for doneness. The internal temperature should be at 165 degrees for safe consumption. If needed, roast for an additional 10 minutes. Spoon some of the chicken juices over the veggies and chicken and sprinkle with chopped parsley before serving.

Bacon & Cider Brussels Sprouts

1 LB Brussels Sprouts, washed, trimmed and halved
3 slices of Bacon, chopped
¼ cup Red Onion, sliced
1 ½ Tbsp Olive Oil
1 Tbsp Brown Sugar
2 Tbsp Apple Cider Vinegar
¼ cup Apple Cider or Juice
1 tsp Fresh Thyme or ½ tsp of Dried Thyme
Salt & Pepper

Preheat the oven to 425 degrees. Add Brussels sprouts to a baking sheet and toss with olive oil, salt, and pepper. Arrange the sprouts, cut side-down, and roast for 15 minutes.

Remove pan from oven, toss, and roast for another 8 to 10 minutes.

While the sprouts are roasting, start to cook chopped bacon in a pan. When fat is rendered, and bacon is almost done, add in red onion. Sauté for 2 minutes before adding brown sugar, ACV, cider or juice, and thyme. Stir to combine and bring to a bubble. Remove from heat.

Remove Brussels sprouts from the oven and toss with bacon mixture in a pan to coat before serving.

Smoked Gouda Mac & Cheese

12 oz Elbow Pasta, dry weight
¼ cup (1/2 stick) Unsalted Butter
¼ cup AP Flour
2 ½ cups Milk
½ Tbsp Spicy Mustard
2 tsp Paprika, divided
6 oz Smoked Gouda, shredded
5 oz Mild Cheddar, shredded
¾ cup Breadcrumbs
1 Tbsp Olive Oil
Salt
Black Pepper

It's best to grate your own cheese when making cheese sauces. Packaged shredded cheese is coated with potato starch and/or powdered cellulose to keep it from sticking together in the package. This coating also prevents it from melting well in sauces.

In a pot, bring a pot of salted water to a boil and cook pasta to al dente according to the package directions. Drain when done. Preheat the oven to 350 degrees. In a small bowl, combine breadcrumbs, half of the paprika and olive oil. Mix well and set aside.

In another pot, melt butter over medium heat and whisk in flour to create a roux. Cook for 2-3 minutes and slowly begin to add milk while whisking. Once all the milk has been added, whisk in half the paprika and the spicy mustard. Continuously stir to prevent the flour from settling and sticking to the bottom of the pan. When the milk mixture has heated and is starting to thicken, add in the cheese and whisk to combine thoroughly. When the cheese is fully melted, remove from heat, season with salt & pepper to taste and stir in pasta. Pour into a baking dish and sprinkle with breadcrumb mixture. Bake in the oven for 15-20 minutes.

Chicken Enchilada Soup

This soup is perfect for a chilly or rainy day and what's even better is that you only need one pot! Customize it by adding diced avocado to add a creamy bite, sliced jalapeno for spice, or tortilla strips for some crunch. I love to finish mine with crema and cilantro. It's also easy to make this dish vegan or vegetarian.

2 Tbsp Butter
2 Tbsp AP Flour
2 ½ cups Chicken or Vegetable Broth
2 Tbsp Chili Powder
2 tsp Smoked Paprika
1 tsp Garlic Powder
2 tsp Cumin
½ tsp Oregano
1 small Red Bell Pepper
¼ cup Yellow Onion, small dice
½ LB Chicken Breast or Thighs
2 Tbsp Olive Oil
1 14 ounce can of Black Beans, drained
1 ½ cups Fresh or Frozen Corn Kernels
2 ounces Half & Half
Juice of ½ a lime
Crema (I recommend Cacique)
Chopped Cilantro, garnish
Salt & Pepper

Optional Toppings: Sliced Jalapeno, Diced Avocado, Tortilla Strips

In a large soup pot, heat olive oil over medium-high heat. Sprinkle chicken with salt and half of the smoked paprika. Sear on one side for 3 minutes and cook for an additional 2 minutes on the opposite side. Remove from the pot and set aside. In the same pot, add butter to melt before, and then add in peppers and onions. Cook for 2 minutes and add flour. With a wooden spoon or spatula stir to combine. Continue to cook, stirring continuously for 2-3 minutes. Slowly begin to add the chicken or vegetable broth as you continue to stir. Once all the liquid has been added, you can begin adding spices and herbs. Reduce the heat to medium-low and simmer for 20 minutes. While the broth is simmering, dice the chicken and add to the pot. It will continue to cook to the proper temperature as the soup simmers. Next, rinse and drain the black beans before adding them and the corn to the soup. Continue to simmer for an additional 10 minutes after adding the beans and corn. Add fresh lime juice and the half & half and stir to combine. Adjust to taste with salt & pepper. Serve with crema and chopped cilantro.

Corn & Bacon Chowder

A perfect way to warm up in cooler months!

4 cups of Sweet Corn Kernels (fresh preferably, but frozen works in a pinch)
8 oz of Bacon, cooked, then chopped, reserve 2 Tbsp. of the rendered fat
2 Tbsp Unsalted Butter
1 tsp Garlic, minced
1 Shallot, diced
½ of a Red Bell Pepper, diced (If you'd like to spice it up, substitute with a small jalapeno instead)
4 Tbsp AP Flour
2 cups Chicken or Vegetable Broth
2 ½ cups Milk
1 lb Idaho Potatoes, peeled and diced into 1 ½ inch cubes
½ tsp Dried Thyme
½ tsp Red Pepper Flakes
½ cup Half & Half
½ tsp White Pepper
Salt

Chopped Scallions, optional

Cook off bacon in the oven on a baking sheet or in a pan on the stove until crispy. Roughly chop and set aside. In a large pot set over medium-high heat, add 2 tablespoons of the reserved bacon fat and the butter to melt. When fats have melted add bell pepper, shallot, and garlic and sauté for 1 minute. Next, add in flour and stir continuously for 2 minutes. Add broth, milk and potatoes, thyme, and pepper flakes. Reduce heat to medium low. You want to see a gentle boil here. Stir in a bit of salt and pepper. Cover and simmer for 25-30 minutes. Potatoes should still have their shape and not be completely broken down. At 25 minutes, test potatoes for doneness. Add in corn kernels and continue to cook for 5 minutes more. Stir in Half & Half and bacon. Adjust salt if needed. Top with chopped scallions to serve.

Summer Squash Casserole

3 medium sized Yellow Squash
3 medium sized Zucchini
2 cups Half & Half
3 large Eggs
½ cup Parmesan Cheese
½ tsp Salt
¼ tsp Black Pepper
¼ tsp Dried Basil
½ cup Breadcrumbs
1 Tbsp Olive Oil
1 tsp Paprika

Preheat the oven to 350 degrees. Grease a baking dish with 1 teaspoon of oil. Mix the breadcrumbs with the olive oil and paprika. Wash and slice vegetables evenly into rounds. Place into a baking dish alternately so that colors are visible. Blend the ½ & ½ with the eggs, salt, pepper, and basil. Pour mixture over the squash. Top with parmesan cheese and breadcrumbs. Bake for 30-35 minutes. Let the casserole set for 10 minutes before serving.

Easy Like Sunday Roast

Getting dinner on the table will be a breeze with this low-maintenance recipe!

4 LB Chuck Roast
2 Tbsp Olive Oil
1 LB Baby Carrots
2 LBS Baby Gold Potatoes, cut in half
8 oz Package Pearl Onions
6 Garlic Cloves
2 cups Beef Broth
¼ c Dry Red Wine like Cabernet
3 Sprigs of Thyme
1 cup Frozen Peas
3 Tbsp Cornstarch
3 Tbsp Water
Salt
Pepper

Heat a pan over medium-high heat with olive oil. Season the chuck roast with salt and pepper and sear on all sides for 3-4 minutes each for a deep sear. Add roast, potatoes, carrots, onions, garlic, broth, wine, and thyme to the crockpot. Turn on high and allow to cook for 5 hours. At the end of the 5 hours, mix the cornstarch and water. Gently stir this into the liquid and remove thyme sprigs. Cook for another 30 minutes before adding peas. Set a timer for 15 minutes, and then dinner is done. You may top with parsley to garnish before serving.

I love to serve this roast with homemade biscuits!

If you prefer to put this in the oven, cook at 300 degrees in a Dutch oven or roasting pan covered tightly with layers of parchment paper and aluminum foil.

Homemade Marinara

2 tablespoons Olive Oil
¼ cup Yellow Onion, diced
1 Tbsp garlic, minced
1 cup Water
28 oz can Peeled San Marzano Tomatoes, diced
½ tsp dried oregano
4 large, Fresh Basil Leaves
2 teaspoons sugar
Salt
Pepper
Optional: 1 ½ teaspoon Chili Flakes

In a medium saucepan, heat olive oil over medium heat, add onion and garlic and sauté until fragrant, about 1 minute. Add water, tomatoes, oregano, basil, and sugar, and chili flakes if using. Stir to combine. Turn heat down to low and simmer for 35 minutes. Season with salt and pepper to taste.

At this point the sauce is done. Personally, I prefer a smoother marinara sauce, so I put mine in the blender and process for a few seconds. If you enjoy a chunkier sauce, then you can use it as is.

For a hearty sauce: Brown your choice of ground meat. I like to use a mix of angus beef and veal. Season with salt and pepper. Add the meat to the sauce and simmer for 20 minutes.

Hearty Bolognese Sauce

Roasted Vegetable Lasagna

I first made this for the Hillel house on one of the college campuses nearby. Because it had to be a Kosher meal but still filling and delicious, I chose to combine three of my favorite things: roasted vegetables, cheese, and pasta! Use my homemade marinara for this recipe.
1 medium sized Eggplant, diced into 1-inch cubes. I use it without peeling but you can do whatever you like here.

2 Bell Peppers, diced into 1-inch pieces: Red, Orange, or Yellow
1 each: medium Zucchini and Yellow Squash, diced into 1-inch pieces
2 Tbsp Olive Oil
Salt & Pepper
16 oz Ricotta Cheese
¾ cup Parmesan Cheese
½ pound freshly grated Mozzarella Cheese
12 no boil Lasagna Pasta sheets
Homemade Marinara (see previous recipe)
3 Tbsp chopped Basil

Preheat the oven to 425 degrees.

Dice all vegetables and toss with olive oil, salt, and pepper. Place on a baking sheet and roast for 20 minutes. While you wait for the vegetables to roast, bring a pot of heavily salted water to boil to soak pasta. Combine ricotta, ¼ parmesan, ½ teaspoon of salt, ½ teaspoon of black pepper, and 1 tablespoon basil and mix well. Mix the remaining parmesan with mozzarella. Remove water from heat and soak pasta sheets for 5 minutes.

In a 9X13 baking dish, place a thin layer of marinara sauce on bottom and line with 3 of the pasta sheets.

Layer the pasta and fillings evenly for 3 layers (about 1/3 cup each) starting with marinara followed by roasted vegetables, then ricotta mixture and mozzarella. Repeat two more times, pressing lightly between each layer. For the final layer, top with the remaining pasta sheets and finish with marinara and mozzarella-parmesan mix.

Cover the pan with aluminum foil and bake for 30-35 minutes. Check the lasagna at the 30-minute mark by poking with a small knife or skewer. If the noodles are tender remove foil and broil for 4-5 minutes to achieve a bubbly golden-brown crust. If noodles are not quite done, continue cooking covered for an additional 5 minutes before browning.

Shrimp & Asparagus Risotto

1 Shallot, on the larger side
½ stick Unsalted Butter
2 cups Arborio Rice
1 cup Dry White Wine
6-8 cups Chicken or Vegetable Broth, warmed
½ cup grated Parmesan
½ pound 16/20 Shrimp, peeled & deveined
1 bundle small/medium Asparagus, trimmed
Salt & Pepper

To add more depth of flavor, I like to grill or broil my asparagus before cutting them into 1" pieces. Add to risotto the last 2-3 minutes of cooking. You could also switch out the asparagus for peas. This recipe could also be made vegan by replacing the butter with olive oil or a plant-based butter, plant-based parm and omitting the shrimp. Try adding in sauteed mushrooms and thyme instead of asparagus for a delicious alternative!

In a large saucepan over medium heat, heat half of the butter and sauté the shallots until translucent. Add the rice and stir to coat in butter, for 1 minute. Add the white wine and cook this for about 5 minutes until reduced. Begin to add the warmed broth one cup at a time. Cook until most of the liquid has been absorbed before adding another cup of liquid. Continue to cook and add broth alternatively until the rice is al dente, meaning it should still have a little bite when chewing. Only add liquid as needed. The whole process should take about 20-23 minutes. Season to taste towards the end of cooking with salt & pepper. If using raw asparagus, add to risotto 15 minutes into the cook. Add shrimp to risotto during the last 6-8 minutes of cooking. Once the rice is done and the shrimp are cooked through, remove from heat and stir in remaining butter and parmesan. Adjust seasoning if needed.

Greek Seasoning Blend
Perfect on chicken or vegetables!

2 tsp Dried Oregano
2 tsp Dried Basil
1 tsp Dried Parsley
1 tsp Onion Powder
1 tsp Garlic Powder
½ tsp Thyme
1 tsp Black Pepper
2 tsp Salt

Combine all ingredients and mix well.

I use this blend to make a marinade for chicken. To make the marinade, add the mixture to ¼ cup of olive oil, 1 tablespoon of sugar or honey, and 3 tablespoons of red wine vinegar. Mix well. This also serves as a super easy salad dressing, so be sure to set some aside! Toss the chicken in the marinade and allow it to sit, covered for at least 30 minutes. Grill, bake, or roast chicken and serve with turmeric rice and a salad.

For a Greek inspired salad, chop 1 head of romaine, 3-4 Roma tomatoes, 1 English cucumber, 3 pepperoncini peppers, and ½ a red onion. Add ½ cup each feta and black olives and mix with the reserved marinade mixture.

Turmeric Rice

1 cup Jasmine Rice
1 ¾ cups Chicken or Vegetable Broth
2 tsp Turmeric Powder
¼ tsp Onion Powder
½ tsp Garlic Powder
½ tsp Black Pepper
1 tsp Dried Parsley
Salt, optional

Rinse rice in cold water in a mesh strainer until the water runs clear. In a small pot on medium-low heat, whisk together broth and all seasonings except salt. Add rice and cover. Simmer for 15 minutes. Fluff with a fork and add salt if necessary.

Shrimp Scampi & Linguine

This is one of my favorite dishes to make! It's simple, delicious and takes very little time to put together. For the best results, I recommend using fresh linguini found at specialty stores or in common grocery stores in the refrigerated section. This is usually in the deli section of most grocery stores.

9 oz Linguini, uncooked
½ pound 16/20 Shrimp
¾ stick Unsalted Butter
4 Tbsp Olive Oil
1 diced Shallot
2 Tbsp minced Garlic
1 cup Dry, White Wine
½ tsp Red Pepper Flakes
Salt & Pepper
½ Lemon
Chopped Parsley for garnish, optional

In a pot bring water and a generous sprinkle of salt to a gentle boil. While you wait for the water to boil, heat a skillet over medium-high heat and add butter and olive oil. When the butter is melted, stir in shallot and garlic. Cook for 1 minute and then add wine. Allow the wine to reduce by cooking for 3-4 minutes. You may start to cook the pasta when you start the shrimp. After the wine has reduced, add shrimp, red pepper flakes, salt, and pepper. Cook shrimp for 1 ½ minutes on one side, flip, and cook for 1 ½ minutes more on the other side. Remove shrimp and sauce from heat and drain pasta. Place pasta in a large pasta bowl. Pour sauce and shrimp over pasta and squeeze juice from half a lemon over the dish.

Sprinkle with parsley and serve.

Pair with a light-bodied white wine such as Pinot Grigio or Grenache Blanc and the Garlic Drop biscuits that follow.

Garlic Drop Biscuits

2 ½ cups Self-Rising Flour
¼ cup Vegetable Shortening
½ tsp Salt
1 tsp Sugar
½ cup Sharp Cheddar Cheese
2 tsp Garlic Powder
2/3 cup Low-Fat Buttermilk
6 Tbsp Unsalted Butter
¼ tsp Paprika
A dash or two of Cayenne Pepper

Preheat the oven to 425 degrees. Combine flour, shortening, salt, sugar, and cheese, and 1 tsp of garlic powder by hand until the flour mixture has a sandy consistency. Slowly begin to mix in buttermilk by hand or with a wooden spoon. Once all the liquid has been combined, let the mixture sit in the refrigerator for 10-15 minutes to chill.

Line a baking sheet with parchment paper or smear a thin coat of shortening across the bottom. Using a 2-ounce scoop, scoop out biscuits. Bake for 14-16 minutes. While biscuits are baking, melt butter and mix with remaining garlic powder, cayenne and paprika. When biscuits are done, remove from the oven and let cool for 5 minutes. Brush with butter mixture and serve warm.

The Story

My grandma Lulu served these pineapple sweet potatoes at every holiday meal when I was growing up, and they were always my favorite thing on the plate. She was a fantastic cook who made her mark in Morrisville, N.C., with her restaurant and hair salon. She knew everyone, and everyone knew her. She was small in stature, but her personality was as big as the sky. She was funny, passionate, direct, and stubborn. Strong and sassy. A Virgo in every way. I knew that I had to include this recipe as a tribute to my late grandma, who I love and miss so very much.

Lulu's Sweet Potatoes

4 medium-sized Sweet potatoes
3 Tbsp Unsalted Butter
1/3 cup Sugar or To Taste
18 oz can Crushed Pineapple, drained

Preheat the oven to 400 degrees. Wash any dirt from the sweet potatoes. On an aluminum lined pan place and roast the sweet potatoes until tender throughout, about 50 minutes. If sweet potatoes are not completely cooked, allow them to cook for 10 minutes more.

Remove potatoes from the skin and place in a mixing bowl. I like to blend my sweet potatoes with an immersion blender to make them silky smooth, but you can just mash them as well. Mix in sugar, butter, and pineapple. Combine thoroughly. Adjust sweetness to your liking. Bake for 10 minutes. There are members of my family who prefer this dish a little sweeter than I do, so feel free to play with the amount of sugar used. If for health or other reasons you are watching your sugar intake, start by mixing in half the amount to begin with. These can be served the same day or 1-2 days after, as the flavors are even better and they are easy to reheat.

Hot Honey Pork Chops

1 cup Self-Rising Flour
1 ¼ tsp Salt
½ tsp Black Pepper
1 tsp Paprika
½ tsp Garlic Powder
1 cup Buttermilk
4 to 6 Boneless Pork Chops, about ½ inch thick
2-3 cups Canola Oil
¼ cup chopped Cilantro

For the Hot Honey:
⅓ cup Honey of good quality
1- 1 ½ Tbsp Sriracha

Preheat oil in a fryer or deep pot to 365 degrees. Whisk together flour, salt, pepper, paprika, and garlic powder in one shallow dish and the milk into another dish. Dip each pork chop in the flour mix, coating both sides. Then, dunk each side into the buttermilk and back into the flour mixture.

Carefully drop pork chops into heated oil and fry for 6-8 minutes, working in two batches. Place cooked pork chops on a wire rack to drain excess oil. Keep the oil temperature between 350-365 degrees to ensure proper cooking.

As you wait for chops to cook, mix the sriracha and honey to combine. Drizzle pork chops with sriracha honey and sprinkle with cilantro before serving.

For a comforting and delicious meal, serve with smoked gouda mac & cheese.

Panko Parmesan Crusted Chicken

4-6 Boneless, Chicken Breasts
8 oz Cream Cheese, softened
3 oz Shredded Parmesan
½ cup Panko Breadcrumbs
½ tsp Paprika
½ tsp Garlic Powder
1/8 tsp Cayenne Pepper
3 Tbsp Olive Oil
Salt
Pepper

Preheat oven to 375 degrees. Prepare the cream cheese mixture by mixing softened cheese with ½ of the parmesan and the cayenne pepper. Mix panko, paprika, and remaining parmesan with 1 tablespoon of olive oil. Set both the cream cheese mixture and breadcrumbs aside until ready to use. Pound chicken breasts with a mallet until they are ½ inch in thickness. Heat oil in a skillet over medium-high heat. Season chicken with salt, pepper, and garlic powder. Sear the first side of the chicken for 2 minutes and flip. Cook for one minute and remove pan from heat.

Transfer the chicken breasts to a parchment lined sheet pan. Divide the cream cheese mixture evenly between the chicken breasts and spread over the top. Sprinkle the breadcrumbs over the cream cheese and place in the oven to allow the chicken to finish cooking and toast the breadcrumbs, about 8-10 minutes. At the 8-minute mark, check the chicken for doneness with a thermometer. The chicken is fully cooked at an internal temperature of 165 degrees.

Serving suggestion: whipped potatoes and roasted asparagus

Spicy Southern Collards

These collard greens have some kick, but if you are not a fan of spicy foods, you can reduce or omit the red pepper flakes. Depending upon the brand of stock that you use, salt may or may not be required. Taste halfway through the cooking process for seasoning.

1 bundle of Fresh Collards, washed, trimmed and chopped
8 oz Smoked Ham or Turkey
¼ cup Red Onion, sliced
1 Tbsp Garlic, minced
3 Tbsp Brown Sugar
¼ cup Apple Cider Vinegar
1 ½ tsp Red Pepper Flakes
32 oz Chicken or Vegetable Stock
Salt, optional

Add everything to a large pot or Crockpot. Mix to combine well. Bring to a boil then cover and simmer for 1-1 ½ hours. If using a crockpot, cook on high for 2 hours. Season with salt if needed.

Roasted Broccolini
with Lemon & Parmesan

2 bunches of Broccolini, washed and trimmed
1 small Lemon
1 ½ Tbsp Olive Oil
1 tsp Garlic, minced
¼ cup Parmesan
Salt & Pepper

Preheat the oven to 400 degrees. In a large bowl, toss broccolini with olive oil, juice of half a lemon, salt, and pepper. Mix well. Place in a single layer on a baking sheet. Roast in the oven for 10-15 minutes. Transfer to a serving dish and sprinkle with parmesan and lemon zest.

Grilled Snapper
with Cilantro Sauce

4-6 skin-on Snapper Filets, 5 oz each
1 ½ tsp Paprika
½ tsp Garlic Powder
½ tsp Chili Powder

1 Tbsp minced Garlic
1/3 cup finely chopped fresh cilantro
1 small Fresno Chili, seeds removed and rough chopped
1 tsp Honey
1/4 cup fresh lime juice
4 Tbsp olive oil
Salt & Pepper

Prepare the cilantro sauce by blending the chopped cilantro with minced garlic, honey, pepper, lime juice, 2 tablespoons of olive oil and salt to taste in a food processor. Set aside until ready to use.

Preheat a large skillet over medium heat with remaining olive oil. Mix paprika, garlic powder, chili powder, ¼ teaspoon of pepper and one tablespoon of salt. Sprinkle over the flesh side of the fish. Begin searing fish, flesh side down for 3 minutes. Sprinkle skin side with seasoning before flipping. Add additional olive oil if needed. Continue to sear fish for 5 minutes. Transfer to a serving platter and top with cilantro sauce.

Corn Relish
This easy accompaniment pairs well with seafood or steak

2 cups Corn Kernels, fresh or frozen
1 small Red Bell Pepper, diced small
¼ cup Yellow Onion, diced small
¼ cup Sugar
¼ Apple Cider Vinegar
3 Tbsp Water
1 tsp Salt
¼ tsp Black Pepper
2 tsp Olive Oil

In a pot over medium-high heat, add the olive oil and onions. Cook for 1-2 minutes to soften the onions a bit. Add the rest of the ingredients to the pot and bring to a boil, stirring to combine. Once the mixture reaches a boil, turn down the heat to medium-low and simmer for 20 minutes. Cool completely before serving. This is best when prepared a couple of days before using.

Smokey Queso Dip

This recipe was inspired by the queso at one of my favorite restaurants. After we moved further out from the city, I couldn't indulge as frequently as I'd wanted to. So, the only obvious solution was to try and create my own! This creamy cheese dip has a smokey profile from the chipotle powder and smoked paprika. Serve with tortilla chips, over burritos or stir into cooked rice to spice up taco night.

½ pound American Cheese
¾ - 1 cup Half & Half
2 tsp Chipotle Powder
1 ½ tsp Smoked Paprika
1 tsp Chili Powder
½ tsp Garlic Powder
1 tsp Ground Cumin
Cilantro, chopped for garnish (optional)

In a saucepan over medium heat, add ¾ cup of milk. When milk starts to warm, add cheese and stir to combine. Stir in spices to mix well. If you would like a thinner queso, add more milk as needed. Transfer queso to a warm bowl or large ramekin and top with chopped cilantro to serve.

Corn & Tomato Salad
with Prosecco Vinaigrette

4 Ears of Yellow Corn, roasted and kernels removed
8 oz Cherry Tomatoes, cut in half
4 slices of cooked Bacon, chopped
2 Tbsp fresh Basil, chopped
1 small Shallot, finely minced
¼ cup Extra Virgin Olive Oil
2 Tbsp Canola Oil
2 ½ Tbsp Prosecco or Champagne Vinegar
3 Tbsp Honey
Salt
Pepper

Sprinkle corn with salt and a bit of olive oil before wrapping in aluminum foil. Roast in the oven for 20 minutes at 425 degrees. You can prepare the vinaigrette while the corn roasts. Mince the shallot and add to a bowl along with the oils, vinegar, honey, ½ teaspoon salt and ¼ teaspoon of pepper. Whisk together until thoroughly combined.

Remove kernels from corn cob and place in a large bowl. In the same bowl, add the bacon, tomatoes, and basil. Start by tossing the salad with half of the vinaigrette. After all of the ingredients are mixed together, give it a taste. Add more of the vinaigrette if desired. Serve at room temperature.

This salad goes well with a perfectly cooked steak or grilled chicken!
Serving Suggestion.

I think about cooking as an artist would think about making music or painting. The spark comes from making other people happy. When I see a little dance after a first bite or overhear whispers of how delicious something is, it makes my heart so happy.

Chef Kita

At some point along my journey, I fell in love with Asian cuisine. Chinese was probably the only Asian food that was available when I was growing up, but imagine my delight when my taste buds discovered Korean kimchi, Vietnamese pho, or Japanese gyoza. It's like a whole new world opened before me. Asian food is so many things, depending on what part of the continent you're referring to. Asia is divided into provinces: North, South, East, West, Southeast, and Central, and each has its own style of cooking and is known for specializing in certain dishes.

During the pandemic, I began to practice some of my favorite Asian dishes. Some I became good at, and let's just say some still need a little work. In small ways, I have managed to blend my Southern roots with Asian influences to create some tasty bites featured in this section. Don't worry, there's nothing too complicated here. Even a new cook can create a little taste of Asia in their very own kitchen.

Asian Influences

Sriracha Aioli

I love to add this as a topping for my Korean short rib tacos, but it also goes well with burgers, as a dipper for fries or chicken tenders! This can be stored in an airtight container in the fridge for up to 2 weeks.

½ cup Mayonnaise
3 Tbsp Sriracha
1 tsp Lime Juice
1 ½ tsp Honey

Whisk all ingredients together to combine well.

Napa Slaw

1 small Napa Cabbage
2 Tbsp Cilantro, chopped
2 tsp Sugar
Juice of 1 Lime or 3 Tbsp Lime Juice
¼ tsp Salt

Using a mandolin, shave the cabbage. If you do not have a mandolin, use a sharp knife to thinly shave the cabbage. Toss with sugar, lime juice, cilantro and salt. Mix well. Cover and refrigerate until ready to use.

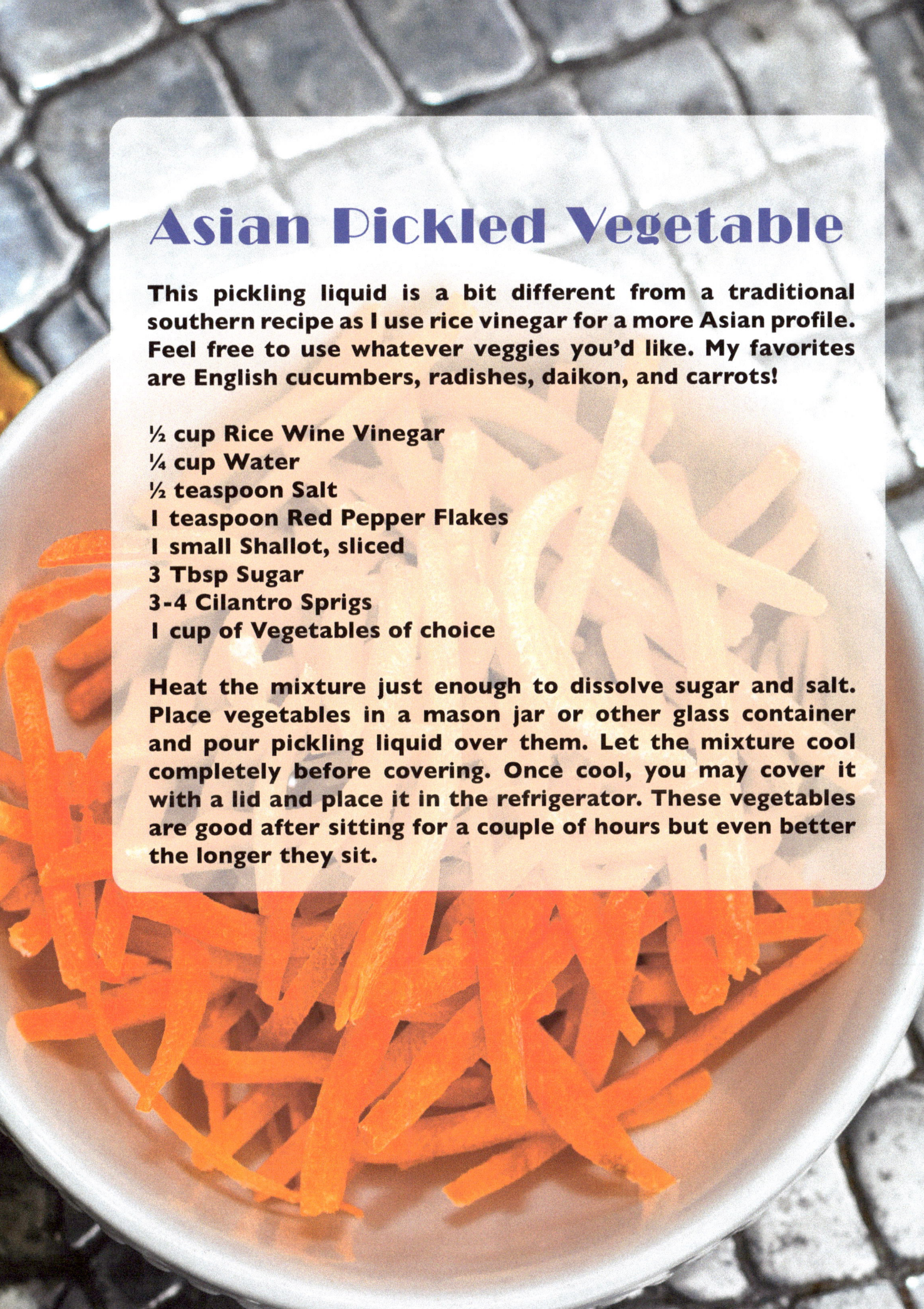

Asian Pickled Vegetable

This pickling liquid is a bit different from a traditional southern recipe as I use rice vinegar for a more Asian profile. Feel free to use whatever veggies you'd like. My favorites are English cucumbers, radishes, daikon, and carrots!

½ cup Rice Wine Vinegar
¼ cup Water
½ teaspoon Salt
1 teaspoon Red Pepper Flakes
1 small Shallot, sliced
3 Tbsp Sugar
3-4 Cilantro Sprigs
1 cup of Vegetables of choice

Heat the mixture just enough to dissolve sugar and salt. Place vegetables in a mason jar or other glass container and pour pickling liquid over them. Let the mixture cool completely before covering. Once cool, you may cover it with a lid and place it in the refrigerator. These vegetables are good after sitting for a couple of hours but even better the longer they sit.

Korean Short Rib Taco Spread

To be honest, this is one of my favorite recipes in this book! I get excited every time I make these short ribs. Serve over steamed jasmine rice with Bok choy or snow peas or over the gouda mac & cheese also featured in the pages of this book. My preference is to create a taco spread, which works perfectly if you're entertaining a crowd. Throw some tortillas on the grill and gather up some toppings. The sriracha aioli, pickled veggies, and napa slaw are great additions to this taco set-up. I also recommend mashed avocado and crumbled queso fresco. Mix up some margaritas, and I'd say that's a recipe for a great time!

Korean Short Ribs

To be honest, this is one of my favorite recipes in this book! I get excited every time I make these short ribs. Serve over steamed jasmine rice with Bok choy or snow peas or over the gouda mac & cheese also featured in the pages of this book. My preference is to create a taco spread, which works perfectly if you're entertaining a crowd. Throw some tortillas on the grill and gather up some toppings. The sriracha aioli, pickled veggies, and napa slaw are great additions to this taco set-up. I also recommend mashed avocado and crumbled queso fresco. Mix up some margaritas, and I'd say that's a recipe for a great time!

5 pounds of Bone-In Short Ribs, 1-2 inch thick
6 Cloves of Garlic
3 1-inch pieces of Ginger
½ Yellow Onion, roughly chopped
32 ounces Beef Broth
Olive Oil
Salt
Pepper

For the Sauce:
1/2 cup Apple Juice
¾ cup Tamari
1 cup Light Brown Sugar
2 Tbsp Fresh Ginger, grated or ¾ Tbsp Dry Ginger
2 Tbsp minced Garlic
¼ cup Mirin
2 Tbsp Sesame Oil
1 ½ Tbsp Rice Wine Vinegar
2 Tbsp Gochugang
3 Tbsp Water
3 Tbsp Cornstarch
1 Tbsp Sesame Seeds

A large Dutch oven is recommended for this recipe. If you don't have one, a roasting pan will work. Preheat the oven to 275 degrees. Heat a few tablespoons of olive oil in a Dutch oven or skillet on medium-high heat. Season all sides of the short ribs with salt & pepper. Working in batches begin to sear the meat on all sides for about 1 1/2 – 2 minutes each and set to the side. Once the meat is all seared, add a bit of olive oil to the pan and sauté the onion, ginger, and garlic for 2 minutes.

Remove from heat and place the short ribs back into the Dutch oven with the vegetables and pour in the beef broth. If you are using a roasting pan, wrap tightly with layers of parchment paper and aluminum foil. Place in the oven and set a timer for 3 ½ hours.

In a pot, combine all the ingredients except for the water, cornstarch, and sesame seeds. On medium-high heat whisk the ingredients together. In a small bowl mix the water and cornstarch. As the sauce mixture in the pot comes to a boil, whisk in the cornstarch and water mix, known as a slurry. The sauce will begin to thicken. Remove from heat after a minute and stir in sesame seeds.

Check the ribs for tenderness at the end of the timer. They should pull away from the bone quite easily. If this is not the case, cover and continue to cook for an additional 20-30 minutes. Reheat the sauce until warm. Transfer the short ribs to a serving platter and spoon sauce over them.

Reserve broth used to cook short ribs for later use. Allow it to cool and skim off fat. Liquid can be stored in the refrigerator for up to 7 days or in the freezer for a month. Use the liquid to make gravy, stew or soup.

Sweet Chili Sauce

½ cup Rice Wine Vinegar
½ cup Water
½ cup Sugar
1 Tbsp Dry Sake
1 Tbsp Fish Sauce
1 Tbsp Tamari
1 Tbsp Gochugang
½ tsp Red Pepper Flakes
1 ½ tsp minced Garlic
1 Tbsp Cornstarch
1 Tbsp Water

Mix cornstarch and water and set it aside. Combine all the other ingredients in a pot and bring to a boil. When it reaches a boiling point, whisk in the slurry, and remove from heat. The mixture will thicken more as it cools. Use as a dipping sauce for spring rolls, eggrolls, or tempura.

Pork Egg Rolls

1 tsp Sesame Oil
8 oz Ground Pork
3 Scallions, chopped
1 Tbsp Garlic, grated
1 Tbsp Garlic, minced
2 cups shaved Cabbage
1 ½ cups shredded Carrots
1 ½ tsp Cornstarch
1 tsp Soy Sauce
1 tsp Hoisin Sauce
Salt
Pepper
1 package of 12 Egg Roll Wrappers
1 Egg, beaten

Brown the ground pork in a pan on medium-high heat, breaking apart as it cooks. Season with a sprinkle of salt. When the pork is thoroughly cooked, remove from pan and drain fat. In the same pan heat the sesame oil and sauté the ginger, garlic, and scallion for 1 minute. Add the rest of the vegetables and the cornstarch to the pan, seasoning with a little salt & pepper. Cook for 3 minutes. Add the soy and hoisin sauces and continue to cook for one minute more. Add ground pork back to the pan and stir to combine well. Remove from heat. Let cool before assembling the egg rolls or you will have a mess!

Open the package of egg roll wrappers and lay out 2-3 at a time to assemble to prevent them from drying out too much. Turn the wrapper diagonally and place about 2 ½ tablespoons of filling in a horizontal line across the center of the wrapper. Fold the sides of the wrapper towards the center. Fold the bottom corner over the filling. Roll tightly, going upwards towards the top corner. Brush the egg on the upper corner and edges to seal. Place the seal side down in a pan.

To Fry: Preheat oil in a pan or deep fryer to 350 degrees. When the oil is hot, very carefully place egg rolls in oil and cook for 3-4 minutes.

To store: Place cooked egg rolls in a freezer bag and freeze for up to 2 months. Place on a baking sheet and bake in an oven preheated to 350 degrees. Bake for 8-9 minutes.

Hoisin Pork Meatballs

1 pound Ground Pork
½ cup Panko breadcrumbs
1 egg
¼ cup Whole Milk
½ tsp Dry Ginger
4 Scallions
2 tsp minced Garlic
1 ½ tsp Salt
1 tsp White Pepper
½ cup Hoisin Sauce
2 Tbsp Brown Sugar
2 Tbsp Water
½ tsp Garlic Powder

Preheat the oven to 475 degrees. Chop scallions separating the whites from the green parts. In a bowl combine ground pork, panko, egg, milk, ginger, white parts of scallions, minced garlic, salt, and pepper. Mix well. Roll into 1 ½ - 2-inch balls. On a parchment lined baking sheet, roast the meatballs for 8-11 minutes until firm. While meatballs are cooking, whisk the hoisin, brown sugar, water, and garlic powder in a medium saucepan on medium-high heat until it comes to a gentle bubble. Transfer cooked meatballs to a serving bowl and pour the hoisin sauce over them. Garnish with green parts of the remaining scallion.

For an easy dinner, serve these delicious meatballs over scallion rice with ponzu green beans. To add some spice, drizzle with sriracha aioli.

Roasted Green Beans
with Ponzu

1 ½ pounds Green Beans, trimmed
¼ cup Ponzu
2 tsp Sesame Oil
½ tsp Salt
½ tsp Black Pepper

Place a baking sheet in the oven and preheat to 400 degrees. Place the beans in a large bowl and toss with ponzu, sesame oil, salt, and pepper. When the oven is ready, take the pan out and dump beans onto it in a single layer. Roast for 10-12 minutes.

Scallion Rice

1 cup dry Jasmine Rice
1 ¾ cup Water
3 Scallions, whites removed and sliced
1 tsp Salt
2 tsp Olive Oil

Rinse rice thoroughly in cold water until the water runs clear. In a small pot heat the olive oil and sauté the scallion whites for 1 minute. Add the rice, water, and salt to the pot. Bring to a boil. Reduce heat to low, cover and simmer for 15 minutes. Fluff with a fork when done.

Sweet & Spicy Soy Glaze

⅓ cup Brown Sugar
½ cup Soy Sauce
¼ cup Mirin
¼ cup Water
1-1 ½ tsp Sriracha
1 Tbsp Cornstarch
1 Tbsp Water

Mix 1 tablespoon of cornstarch with 1 tablespoon of water and set aside. In a small saucepan, whisk together the remaining ingredients on medium-high heat. When the mixture starts to boil, whisk in the cornstarch mixture. Cook for 1 minute and remove from heat.
This is a very versatile sauce that works great for so many things. Use it on veggies, meat, fish, or tofu. Try it in place of the hoisin sauce for the meatballs for a switch.

Thai Steak Lettuce Wraps
with Lime Vinaigrette

1 pound Flank Steak
1 Tbsp Baking Soda
1 cup Cornstarch
¼ cup Soy Sauce
2 Tbsp Mirin
1 tsp Dry Ginger
Canola Oil for wok
2 Tbsp minced Garlic
¼ cup julienned Red Onion
½ cup sliced Red Bell Pepper
½ cup sliced Green Bell Pepper
1-2 sliced Thai or Fresno Chiles
8-10 Iceberg Lettuce pieces
¼ cup chopped Cilantro

Prep vegetables by slicing peppers and onions and mincing garlic. Wash lettuce and cilantro and pat dry. Chop cilantro and set aside.

Slice steak into thin pieces. It is helpful to put the steak in the freezer for 20 minutes beforehand and use a very sharp knife to slice the steak. Place in a bowl when cut and sprinkle with the baking soda. Add 2 cups of cold water and stir gently. Let this sit while you make the vinaigrette.

Combine all ingredients for the vinaigrette and whisk well to dissolve sugar. Set it aside.

Drain the water from the steak and pat dry. Place steak in a bowl and add soy sauce, mirin, and ginger. Mix with hand. Add ¼ cup of oil to the wok to heat. Coat steak in cornstarch. Working quickly, cook the steak in batches. Stir fry for 2-3 minutes and use a skimmer to remove. Drain on a paper towel. Once all the steak has been cooked, add the peppers and onions to the pan. Sprinkle with ½ teaspoon of salt and pepper. Sauté for 2 minutes, then add garlic. Continue to sauté for 1 minute more. Return the cooked steak pieces to the pan and stir to combine. Remove from heat and transfer the mix to a large bowl. Pour some of the vinaigrette over the steak and vegetables and top with chopped cilantro. Serve alongside torn lettuce pieces.

Pineapple Fried Rice

2 cups Cooked Jasmine Rice, cold
2 Tbsp Canola Oil
2 tsp Chili Oil
2 Eggs
¼ cup Shredded Carrots
1 Small Shallot, diced
4 Scallions, chop and separate white parts from the green parts
1 Fresno Chili, diced
1 cup Chopped Napa Cabbage
1 cup diced Pineapple
2 Tbsp Dark Soy Sauce
1 Tbsp Oyster Sauce
¼ cup chopped Cilantro
Salt

Prep all your vegetables before you start to cook. This will make it easier for you to work quickly and prevent you from burning anything. Heat a wok or large skillet with the oils over medium-high heat. Add the shallots, diced chili, and white parts of the scallions and cook for 1 minute before adding rice. Using a spatula, break up the cold rice and add the 2 eggs, stirring to coat the rice. Add the carrots, cabbage, and pineapple and continuously stir to cook the vegetables for 5 minutes. Add soy sauce and oyster sauce and stir to combine thoroughly, being sure to scrap the bottom. Adjust seasoning with salt if needed and top with cilantro and green scallion parts.

Kita's KFC
(Korean Fried Chicken)

2 pounds of Chicken, I prefer wings and drumsticks, but this is entirely up to you

For the marinade:
½ cup Soy Sauce
1 Tbsp Grated Ginger or 2 tsp Dry Ginger

Dry Batter:
1 cup AP Flour
1 cup Cornstarch or Tapioca Flour
2 tsp Paprika
2 tsp Salt

For the Sauce:
3 Tbsp Brown Sugar
4 Tbsp Honey
4 Tbsp Dark Soy Sauce
1 Tbsp Sesame Oil
2 tsp Paprika
2 tsp minced Garlic
1-2 tsp Gochugaru or 1-2 Tbsp Gochugang

Optional: Chopped Cilantro or Scallions for garnish

Place the chicken and the marinade ingredients into a large bowl and toss to combine using your hands. Cover and refrigerate overnight. If you plan on using it the same day, the chicken can remain covered and on a counter for up to 30 minutes.

Next, it's time to prepare the sauce. In a small saucepan, whisk together the ingredients for the sauce over medium-low heat until the sugar has dissolved and the mixture is bubbling gently. Start with the smallest amount of gochugaru or gochujang and adjust the spice level to your liking. If you are not a fan of spicy food, you can omit this ingredient altogether. Turn the heat to low to keep sauce warm while you fry the chicken.

I prefer to use a deep fryer for this step, but if you don't have one, using a large pot filled with enough oil to cover the chicken (about 4-5 cups) with a thermometer works.

Preheat the oil to 360 degrees. Mix the ingredients for the dry batter in a large bowl or container. Remove the chicken from the marinade, put into the flour mixture, and coat the chicken well. Prepare a rack placed over a pan to drain the chicken. When the oil is ready, very carefully drop the chicken into the hot oil. Chicken wings generally take about 8-10 minutes, and chicken legs about 14-16 minutes to fully cook. Allow longer cooking times for thighs and breasts.

Korean chicken is known for its superbly crispy skin. If you want the full experience, you can fry your chicken pieces once more for 1-2 minutes once you have completed frying all your chicken. Double frying really guarantees an incredibly crispy bite.

Once you are done frying, coat your chicken in the warm sauce and toss well to coat. Sprinkle with cilantro or scallions if using before serving.

Korean Braised Potatoes

1 pound Yukon Potatoes
2 Tbsp Canola Oil
3 Scallions, chopped
1 Red Bell Pepper, diced into 1-inch pieces
¼ cup Soy Sauce
2 Tbsp Mirin
¼ cup Honey
2 Tbsp minced Garlic
1 tsp Sesame Oil
½ Tsp Paprika
½ - 1 tsp Gochugaru
½ Tbsp Oyster Sauce
⅔ cup Water

Heat the olive oil in a pot over medium-high heat. Brown the potatoes in the oil, stirring occasionally until they are golden brown. In the same pot, add the vegetables and the rest of the ingredients. Turn the heat down to low and stir the contents to combine. Simmer until potatoes are tender. Serve at room temperature.

Gochugang Chicken & Vegetables

1 Small Napa Cabbage, Chopped
1 cup Shredded Carrots
4 Green Onions, chopped (separate green and white parts)
½ pound Chicken Breasts, sliced into thin strips
2 Tbsp minced Garlic
3 Tbsp Dark Soy Sauce
1 Tbsp Gochugang
2 Tbsp Honey
2 Tbsp Sesame Oil
¼ cup Apple Juice
2 Tbsp Cornstarch
Salt
2 Tbsp Olive Oil

Heat the olive oil in a wok or skillet over medium-high heat. While waiting for the skillet to heat up, add the garlic, soy sauce, gochujang, honey, sesame oil, and apple juice in a bowl and whisk to combine. Set aside until ready to use. Sprinkle the chicken with salt and place in the skillet to sear. Allow the chicken to cook untouched for 2 minutes.

Add the carrots, cabbage, cornstarch, and sauce mixture to the pan and stir all ingredients together. Allow the sauce to come to a bubble and reduce heat to low. Continue to cook for 2 minutes more and remove from heat. Serve over jasmine rice or any Asian noodles.

Soy-Honey Glazed Salmon

Soy-Honey Glazed Salmon

4 5-ounce Salmon Filets, skin removed
½ cup Honey
1 tsp minced Garlic
½ tsp Dry Ginger
1 ½ Tbsp Soy Sauce
½ tsp Red Pepper Flakes
1 tsp Lime Juice
1 Tbsp Unsalted Butter
1 Tbsp Olive Oil
1 Tbsp Sesame Seeds
Salt
Pepper

Preheat the oven to 400 degrees. In a small bowl combine the honey, garlic, ginger, soy sauce, pepper flakes, and lime juice. Preheat a cast iron or other oven-safe skillet over medium-high heat with the butter and oil. Sprinkle the salmon filets with salt and pepper. When the pan is hot, place the fat side of the fish in the skillet (not the skin side). Cook the salmon for 3 minutes, then flip. Pour the honey-soy sauce over the filets. Place the salmon in the oven for 9-11 minutes. Spoon sauce over filets and sprinkle with sesame seeds before serving.

Can I Make You a Drink?

Cocktail crafting doesn't need to be an intimidating venture filled with obscure ingredients and complex techniques. I believe that everyone should have the chance to enjoy the pleasure of a well-crafted cocktail, and that's precisely what this section is all about. I'm no mixologist, but I have come up with a few adult beverages that are featured at my gatherings quite often. I have included a collection of recipes that are both approachable and delicious, perfect for those just dipping their toes into mixology waters.

Summer Spritz Sangria

2 cups Blueberries
2 medium-sized Peaches, diced into 1/2 -inch cubes
¾ cup Peach Juice, such as Simply Peach
½ cup Peach Vodka
6-8 Basil Leaves
1 Bottle of Sparkling Wine, I tested with Gemma di Luna Sparkling Moscato

Wash fruit thoroughly to remove any debris and dirt. After removing pits from peaches, slice them. Place fruit and basil leaves in a large pitcher. Pour vodka and juice into the pitcher. Top with the bottle of wine. Stir gently.

Serve over ice in wine glasses.

Pineapple Tickle

1 cup Tequila
1 cup Pineapple Juice
¼ cup Simple Syrup
2 Tbsp Szechuan Peppercorns
4 ounces Amaretto
4 ounces Club Soda
4 Maraschino Cherries

Place all the ingredients except for the club soda and amaretto in a pitcher. Chill in the fridge for at least a full day.
Strain the mixture and divide between 4 cocktail glasses. Add ice and top with 1 ounce each of amaretto and the club soda. Garnish with a cherry.

Simple Syrup:
Combine 1 cup of water with 1 cup of sugar. Bring to a boil to dissolve sugar. Let cool and store in a jar or squeeze bottle. Can be kept in the refrigerator for up to 2 months.

Szechuan peppercorns are not actually pepper at all. They are dried berries from an ash tree. It's famous for creating a tingly, numbing effect in the mouth. They have a strong citrus aroma and taste. You can opt to omit them in this beverage if you'd prefer to skip the tingles.

Bourbon Blackberry Lemonade

2 ½ cups Water
1 cup Blackberries
1 ½ cup Simple Syrup
1 cup Lemon Juice
1 cup Bourbon
Bitters

In a pitcher, add the blackberries and use a muddler or masher to squash them. Add water, simple syrup, lemon juice, and bourbon. Stir to combine. Pour over ice and add a dash of bitters to finish.

Peach Margarita

Peach Simple Syrup:
2 Cup Peaches
1 cup Water
1 cup Sugar

Margarita Mix:
4 Tbsp Lime Juice
8 Ounces Tequila, I tested with Lunazul
2 ounces Triple Sec
Optional: Rimming Sugar or Salt, lime slices

Mash the peaches and add to a pot with the water and sugar. Bring to a boil, stirring until all the sugar has dissolved. Allow the mixture to cool for 30 minutes. Strain the syrup into a squeeze bottle or measuring cup. You can keep this in the fridge until ready to use. It will be good for 2-3 weeks.

Set up 4 cocktail glasses with ice cubes. If you would like to rim your glasses, use lime to go around the edge of the glass and dip in sugar or salt.

To make the margarita, place the lime juice, tequila, triple sec and 2 ½ ounces of the simple syrup in a cocktail shaker. Shake well to blend and pour over ice. Serve with a lime slice.

Feeling a little spicy? Top this peach margarita with Tajin.

Mimosa, Anyone?

My favorite part about brunch might just be the bottomless mimosas! These easy to make cocktails originated in France and have earned their place at most restaurants that offer a brunch option. They are also featured at bridal showers, midday weddings, and Mother's Day lunches. The varieties are endless, so you could easily switch up the flavor profile to reflect the seasons or to complement your menu. Call (or text) some friends and plan a brunch date. *Have everyone make a dish from the "Let's Do Brunch" section and try out one or all my favorite mimosa variations.*

Mimosa

Orange juice and champagne is the most well-known and classic mix. Sometimes, a splash of Grand Marnier is added. Some people choose to add the sparkling wine first and then top it with juice. I personally prefer the opposite. I add 2.5 ounces of juice to a champagne flute and then top with Prosecco.

To make: Pour 2.5 ounces of juice and top with Prosecco.

Peach Mimosa: Peach Juice like Simply Peach
Apple Crisp: Apple Cider + 1 Tbsp Brandy
Lychee Saki-mosa: Lychee Puree + 1 Tbsp Sake
The Poinsettia: Simply Cranberry Juice
Pineapple Mimosa: Simply Pineapple Juice + 1 tsp Grenadine

Staying away from alcohol? No problem! Substitute the champagne with sparkling cider, ginger beer, or sparkling water.

Sweet Endings

Sweet Endings

You've had a journey through my kitchen and here we are at the final stop-the sweet spot! I've taken some of the classics of the south and infused them with a little creativity.

The South is famous for its warm hospitality, and nothing expresses that better than a beautifully crafted dessert. From pecan pies that embody the essence of Southern pecan groves to the silky smoothness of chess pie, this region boasts a treasure trove of sweet traditions passed down through generations.

Whether you're a seasoned baker or a dessert novice, you'll find something to satisfy your sweet tooth and inspire your inner pastry chef.

Coconut Vanilla Bread Pudding
with Anglaise

So, this recipe kind of happened by accident. I made the first variation of this one day at work while attempting to make a dessert out of scraps of brioche that I didn't want to go to waste. I accidentally grabbed the coconut extract instead of vanilla when I was making the custard for a bread pudding. I realized it as soon as I began to pour the extract. I happen to love all things coconut, so I figured it would still turn out pretty good. The first bite was even better than I expected! I've tweaked it here and there over the years to what I believe is a coconut lover's dream.

1 pound of Brioche
4 large Eggs
3 cups Heavy Cream
1 cup Coconut Milk
1 ¼ cup Sugar
¾ cup Shredded Coconut
2 tsp Vanilla Paste
2 Tbsp Unsalted Butter

Bread puddings work best with bread that has been dried out a bit. You will want to dice the bread into 1" squares a day ahead. Place the bread on a sheet pan and place in an oven that is not on and leave overnight to help remove some of the moisture.

When you are ready to make the pudding, use the butter to grease a baking dish. Place the cubed bread and shredded coconut into the baking dish. Blend the heavy cream, coconut milk, eggs, vanilla paste, and sugar using an immersion or stand blender. Pour this mixture over the bread and coconut. Let the bread soak in the custard mixture for at least an hour before baking. Preheat the oven to 350 degrees before putting the bread pudding in the oven. Bake for 35 to 45 minutes. The pudding should be a little wobbly in the center with browned edges when done. It will continue to set as it cools. Pour the anglaise over the bread pudding before serving.

Anglaise

Anglaise or Crème Anglaise is a cream sauce that is used in or poured over many desserts. It's very common to have this served as a sauce for bread pudding. It's made from egg yolks, cream, sugar, and vanilla. Some even have the addition of liqueur. Try this anglaise drizzled over French toast, pound cake, or fruit.

You can make this while you wait for the bread pudding to bake.

2 Egg Yolks
1 cup Cream
1/3 cup Sugar
1 Tbsp Vanilla Extract

In a glass or stainless-steel bowl, whisk the eggs and sugar together until the sugar has dissolved and the mixture is pale yellow in color. Bring the cream and vanilla to a simmer over medium-low heat in a small saucepan, stirring to prevent it from scorching. Once you see a few bubbles along the edge of the pot, it is ready, and you can remove it from the heat. Do not let the cream boil.

You can begin to temper the egg yolks by simultaneously whisking the egg & sugar mixture and adding in the cream a bit at a time. You can begin adding the cream in a slow, steady stream once the mixture has thinned out some.

When all the cream has been combined with the egg, transfer the custard back to the pan and cook over low heat. Stir constantly for about 5 minutes. The sauce should be thick enough to coat the back of a spoon when done. Strain to remove any bits of egg or sugar.

Place it in a bowl and allow it to cool.

Peach Cobbler

Ginger Peach Cobbler
with Ginger Cream

5 cups Frozen Peaches
1 cup Sugar, divided
1 cup Water
1 Tbsp Vanilla Extract
2 Tbsp Cornstarch

1 Stick Unsalted Butter
1 ¾ cups Self-Rising Flour
1 ¾ cups Sugar
1 cup Whole Milk
1 tsp Cinnamon
½ tsp Nutmeg

For the Ginger Cream:
1 cup Heavy Cream
1 ½ tsp Dry Ginger
2 ½ Tbsp Powdered Sugar

Preheat the oven to 350 degrees. In a large pot, combine the peaches, ½ cup of sugar, water, and cornstarch. Bring to a boil. Turn the heat down to simmer and let cook for 5 minutes.

Melt the butter in a baking dish and set aside. In a separate bowl whisk the flour, cinnamon, remaining sugar, and milk together to create a batter.

Pour the peaches and liquid into the baking dish. Pour the flour mixture over the fruit and put it into the oven. Bake for 35-40 minutes. The edges will be pulled away from the sides and golden brown. Allow the cobbler to cool for 10-15 minutes. Serve in individual bowls with a dollop of ginger cream.

Chocolate Chess Pie

2 ¾ cups Sugar
10 Tbsp Dark Cocoa Powder
4 Tbsp All-Purpose Flour
½ tsp Salt
1 cup Half & Half
6 large Eggs
7 Tbsp Unsalted Butter, melted
2 ½ tsp Vanilla
1 9" pie crust

Preheat the oven to 325 degrees. Whisk the first four ingredients together in a mixing bowl. Blend in the milk and add eggs one at a time. When the eggs have all been added, whisk in the butter and vanilla.

Partially bake the pie crust by placing a piece of parchment paper on top of the crust and then adding dry beans. Bake in the oven for 12 minutes. This helps ensure that the crust is fully cooked when the pie is done.

After removing the crust from the oven, remove the beans and parchment. Place the crust on a baking sheet and pour the filling into the crust. Bake the pie for 55-60 minutes. Allow the pie to cool completely before serving.

Serving Suggestion: serve with fresh, lightly sweetened whipped cream.

Vanilla Pound Cake
with Blueberry-Thyme Glaze

4 sticks Unsalted Butter, softened
3 ½ cups Sugar
9 Eggs, room temp
1 Tbsp Vanilla Paste or Extract
1 tsp Salt
3 ½ cups Cake Flour

Blueberry-Thyme Glaze:
1 cup Fresh or Frozen Blueberries
1 Tbsp Water
1 Tbsp Fresh Thyme Leaves
1 1/4 cup Powdered Sugar
1 tsp Lemon Juice
2-4 Tbsp Milk

Preheat the oven to 325 degrees. Spray a Bundt pan with baking spray and set aside.

Using a mixer with paddle attachment, cream the butter and sugar on high speed for 7 minutes. Lower speed to medium and add eggs one at a time and incorporate well. Add vanilla and salt and mix for 3 minutes.

Using a spatula or spoon, mix in the flour until the batter is smooth and no flour streaks are visible. Pour the batter into the Bundt pan and bake for 60-70 minutes. A toothpick inserted into the cake should come out clean when the cake is done. Set on a wire rack to cool for 10 minutes and then turn the cake out of the pan.

While the cake is cooling, you can begin working on the glaze. In a small saucepan, add the blueberries and water. Cook on medium heat until the berries begin to burst. Be sure to stir to prevent any burn spots. You can mash the berries with a masher or silicone spatula. Set a sieve over a bowl and push the juices through. Discard the skins. In the same bowl add the powdered sugar, thyme leaves, lemon juice, and 2 tablespoons of milk. Whisk until smooth. Adjust the consistency of the glaze with more milk if you would like to have a thinner glaze.

Pour the glaze over the cake. Let sit for at least 10 minutes before cutting.

Lavender-Lemon Cookies

2 ¾ cups All-Purpose Flour
1 ½ cups Sugar
1 tsp Baking Powder
2 sticks Unsalted Butter, melted
2 Eggs
1 tsp Lavender Paste
2 tsp Lemon Zest
1 tsp Vanilla Extract
Pinch of Salt

In a mixer, place melted butter and sugar and mix on medium until the mixture is a little fluffy, about 3 minutes. Add the eggs, extract, zest, and paste. Mix for two minutes on low speed. While that is mixing, in a separate bowl, combine flour, baking powder, and a pinch of salt.

Start to add the flour mix a little at a time to combine. Once the dough has come together, turn off the mixer and scoop the dough out onto a baking sheet. Using an ice cream scoop will guarantee that the cookies are all the same size. Instead of rolling my cookies down, I prefer to press them down into circles that are about ½-inch thick. Chill the cookies for at least 30 minutes before baking.

Bake in an oven preheated to 350 degrees for 11-13 minutes.

PB, Bacon & Chocolate Cookies

As someone who has baked a lot of cookies, I wanted to come up with something different to add to my rotation. These cookies quickly became a hit with my regulars. This salty, sweet treat combines the classic flavors of peanut butter and chocolate with bacon for a bite that's sure to please.

3 cups All-Purpose Flour
1 tsp Salt
1 tsp Baking Powder
1 cup Sugar
1 cup Brown Sugar
1 stick Unsalted Butter
1 cup Peanut Butter
2 Eggs
¾ cup Chocolate Chips
5 strips of Bacon cooked & chopped.

In a mixing bowl, combine sugars, butter, and peanut butter. Mix on low for 3 minutes. In a separate bowl, add the flour, salt, and baking powder. Add eggs one at a time to the creamed sugar. Mix for 1 minute. Begin to slowly add the flour mixture to the sugar and egg mix. Once all the flour has been added and mixed in well, add the chocolate chips and bacon. Stir in to incorporate into the dough.

Scoop out the dough using a 2 ounce ice cream scoop onto a baking pan and press the cookies down to about ½ an inch. Chill for 15 minutes and bake at 350 degrees for 12-14 minutes.

Cookie dough can be frozen in an airtight container for up to 2 months.

Orange Rice Pudding

2 cups cooked Short-Grain Rice like Arborio or Valencia
3 Egg Yolks, room temp
½ cup Sugar
3 cups Half & Half
¼ tsp Salt
1 Tbsp Orange Zest
¼ cup Orange Juice

Cook one cup of short-grain rice until it is al dente. This should be about 10 minutes less than recommended on packaging. Preheat the oven to 325 degrees. While the rice is cooking, combine the rest of the ingredients in a mixing bowl. Whisk or whip thoroughly to dissolve sugar, about 3-4 minutes.

Once the rice has cooked, begin to add the sugar mixture a spoonful at a time to the egg mixture to temper it. Once all the rice has been added to the mixture, stir to combine, and then transfer to a baking dish. Bake for 50-60 minutes. If you are serving warm, allow the pudding to sit for 20-30 minutes before serving. The rice pudding can also be served cold if you prefer.

"A recipe has no soul. You, as the cook, must bring soul to the recipe."

Thomas Keller

Making memories, enjoying life, and

filling their hearts and bellies with love.

Laugh. Eat.

Drink. Repeat!

For interactive cooking videos and more

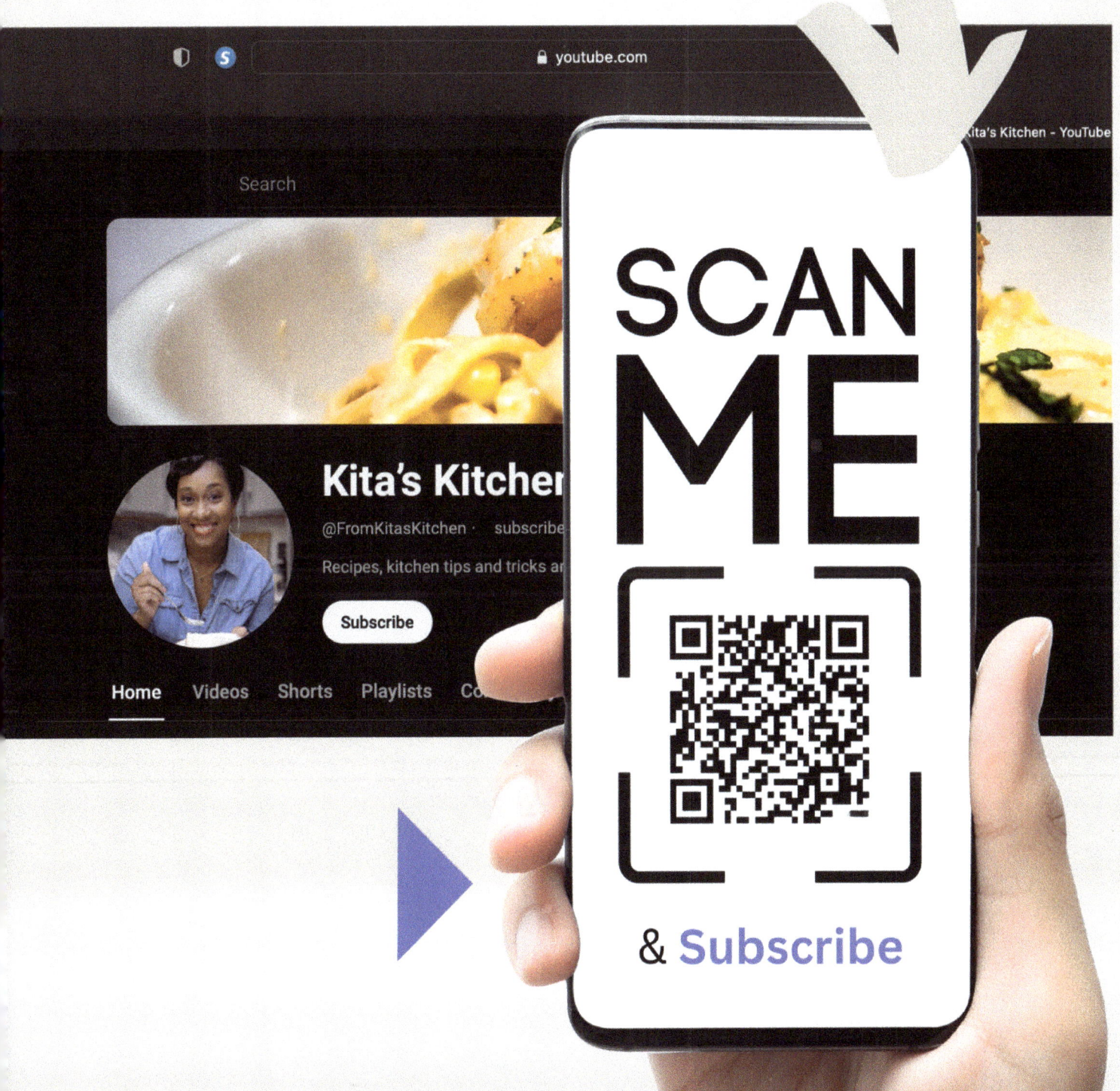

Let's Connect!

f kitaskitchen

📷 fromkitaskitchen

fromkitaskitchen.com

www.ingramcontent.com/pod-product-compliance
Lightning Source LLC
Chambersburg PA
CBHW061407010526
44119CB00011B/284